SoulSync:
30 Days
of
Love and Prayer.

By David Hassan Habbi Love and Lashawnda Love

PUBLISHING

Acknowledgment Page

We want to say a big thank you to our parents, who have always had our backs and showered us with love:

David (Renee Love) Lashawnda (Ervin Flanders and Viola Flanders)

A special shoutout to our wonderful kids – David's 2 and Lashawnda's 3 – you light up our lives!

Big thanks to our awesome brothers and sisters – you know who you are!

And a heartfelt appreciation to our church family, especially Apostle Delesa Patterson and the Kingdom Ambassadors. Your prayers and fellowship mean the world to us.

To everyone else who's been a part of our journey, offering support, love, and good vibes – thank you! We appreciate each and every one of you.

With love and gratitude,

David Hassan Habbi Love and Dr. Lashawnda Love

Introduction:

A Journey of Love and Prayer

Welcome to "SoulSync: 30 Days of Love and Prayer," a heartfelt devotional penned by David Hassan Habbi Love and Dr. Lashawnda Love. Within these pages, we invite you into the sacred space of our marriage, where faith, transformation, and God's grace intertwine.

David and Lashawnda, co-authors and companions in this marital odyssey, extend a warm invitation to join them on a 30-day journey of love and prayer. David, in his inaugural experience of marriage, and Lashawnda, embracing the sacred bond for the third time, offer a unique perspective on the transformative power of love and faith.

Their story is a testament to God's impeccable timing and unchanging love. Within a mere 86 days of meeting, they stood united in marriage—a swift response to their fervent prayers. In the divine orchestration of their lives, God honored the desires of David's heart for a wife and Lashawnda's yearning for a husband.

In the unfolding narrative, their journey took a transformative turn as they embraced God's guidance. Through obedience to His voice and without resorting to pressure or attempts to change, David underwent a profound deliverance—

liberated from the chains of alcohol, cursing, and a street-centric lifestyle.

"SoulSync" is more than a collection of words; it's an intimate sharing of life-altering experiences. As you embark on this 30-day journey, may the words resonate with your soul, bringing inspiration, hope, and a deeper connection with the divine. Just as God honored the prayers of David and Lashawnda, may you too feel His unwavering presence in your journey of love, faith, and transformation.

"SoulSync: 30 Days of Love and Prayer."

Table of Content

Day 1-3:
Communication

Let's dive into a crucial part of marriage – communication. It's like the invisible thread that holds everything together. God made us to communicate, share, and truly get each other through good communication. The Bible talks a lot about using our words right, listening well, and expressing ourselves in a way that shows God's love. Proverbs 18:21 says it clear – "Words can bring life or death." So, here we are, ready for a prayerful journey to make our communication better in this marriage adventure.

Scriptures:

1. **Proverbs 15:1** - "Speak kindly to calm people down, but harsh words stir them up."

2. **Ephesians 4:29** - "Say only what helps, building others up as needed, giving grace to those who hear."

3. **James 1:19** - "Listen more, talk less, and don't get worked up too quickly."

The Importance of Communication (Additional 400 words):

Communication is like the heartbeat of a happy marriage. It's not just about words; it's about really understanding each other and building trust. In a marriage, good communication is the key to getting close and making a strong bond.

Think of communication like the glue that keeps everything together. When we do it right, it sticks us together in a picture of shared dreams, understanding, and support. It's the way we express love, sort out problems, and share our dreams.

Why Good Communication Matters:

1. **Understanding Each Other:** Good communication means really getting each other's thoughts and feelings. It's about creating a space where both of us feel heard and important.

2. **Sorting Out Problems:** Every couple has disagreements, but good communication turns those fights into chances to make things better. When

we communicate openly and respectfully during problems, we find solutions together.

3. **Building Trust:** Trust is like the base of a strong marriage, and good communication is what holds it together. Being open, honest, and clear in communication builds trust bit by bit.

4. **Getting Close:** Through communication, we share our dreams, fears, and what we really want. This sharing creates a deep closeness, making the emotional connection stronger.

5. **Facing Life's Challenges:** Life brings challenges, and good communication is like the compass

that helps us get through them. Whether it's money troubles, health stuff, or family issues, communicating openly and supporting each other is a big deal.

How Bad Communication Causes Problems:

But if we don't communicate well, it can create issues:

1. **Misunderstandings:** If we don't communicate clearly, we might misunderstand each other. Intentions get mixed up, and feelings get hurt.

2. **Growing Apart:** Without good communication, we might start feeling distant emotionally. The connection weakens, and we might drift apart.

3. **Resentment:** If we don't solve problems through communication, bad feelings can build up. Holding onto those emotions can lead to bigger problems later.

4. **More Conflicts:** Bad communication often means more and bigger conflicts. If we struggle to express ourselves, conflicts might get worse instead of getting solved.

5. **Loss of Trust:** Trust fades away when there's no openness and honesty in communication. Keeping secrets or not communicating about worries can make trust break down.

Communication shapes our marriage. It can build us up or tear us down. As we start this journey to make our communication better, let's see how powerful our words can be. May our words bring life, love, and understanding to this special connection we share.

Day 1: *Prayer:* Dear God, we're reaching out for your guidance to make our communication top-notch. Lead us to choose words that bring life and healing to our marriage. Help us be open and honest, creating a safe space to share our hearts. In Jesus' name, we ask for your help. Amen.

Activity: Take a moment today to tell your spouse something positive. Share something you genuinely appreciate about them. This sets the stage for good communication vibes.

Day 2: *Prayer:* Lord, we're aiming for words that reflect love and understanding.

Teach us how to talk in a way that builds up our marriage. Give us the patience to really listen and figure things out. We're counting on you. Amen.

Activity: Practice active listening today. Repeat back what your spouse says to ensure you're on the same page. Look back on your conversation, recognizing their feelings and thoughts.

Day 3: *Prayer:* Heavenly Father, help us listen with kindness and understanding. May our talks be full of grace and kindness. Keep us cool and quick to forgive. Let your love shine in our communication. Amen.

Activity: Write a love note to your spouse. Express why you're grateful they're in your life. It's a simple move but reminds us to be patient and understanding in our talks.

"SoulSync: 30 Days of Love and Prayer."

Keep these ideas rolling throughout the month. Let's build a solid foundation of awesome communication in your marriage, step by step, prayer by prayer.

Day 4-6:
Trust Issues

Let's now discuss trust, which is an essential component of marriage. Trust is like the backbone that supports everything. God designed us to trust, to rely on each other, and to build a solid foundation through trustworthy actions. The Bible echoes the importance of trust, emphasizing that it's something precious and vital. Proverbs 3:5-6 wisely guides us: "Trust in the Lord with all your heart and lean not on your own understanding; in all your ways submit to him, and he will make your paths straight." So, we embark on a prayerful journey to address and rebuild trust within the sacred space of marriage.

Scriptures:

1. **Proverbs 3:5-6 - "Trust in the Lord with all your heart and lean not on your own understanding; in all your ways submit to him, and he will make your paths straight."**

Day 4: How Trust Issues Start

Trust issues often have their roots in misunderstandings, unmet expectations, or past hurts. It could be a breach of confidence, a broken promise, or simply feeling let down. Identifying the source of trust issues is the first step toward healing. As we navigate this day, let's reflect on the moments or events that might have initiated trust issues in our marriage. Understanding the root cause is essential for addressing and resolving trust issues.

Prayer: Dear God, as we explore the beginnings of trust issues, we ask for clarity and insight. Help us understand the roots of any distrust in our marriage. Guide our hearts to a place of openness and honesty as we seek to unravel and address these concerns. In Your name, we pray. Amen.

Activity: Take time to openly discuss with your spouse any past incidents that might have contributed to trust issues. Approach the conversation with a spirit of understanding and a willingness to listen.

Day 5: Dealing with Broken Trust

Broken trust is a painful reality that many couples face. It shatters the foundation, leaving behind feelings of betrayal and hurt. Acknowledging the broken trust is crucial for moving forward. On this day, let's explore the impact of broken trust in our marriage and commit to facing it head-on. Recognizing the pain and seeking resolution are vital steps in the healing process.

Prayer: Heavenly Father, in the face of broken trust, we turn to You for guidance and healing. Grant us the strength to confront the pain and the wisdom to navigate the path of restoration. Help us to forgive and be forgiven, rebuilding what has been broken. Amen.

Activity: Engage in an open and honest conversation about the impact of broken trust. Share your feelings and listen to your spouse's perspective. Begin the process of healing by acknowledging the hurt and expressing a commitment to rebuilding trust.

Day 6: Rebuilding Trust

Rebuilding trust is a journey that requires patience, commitment, and intentional effort. It involves creating a safe space for vulnerability and establishing new patterns of reliability. On this day, let's explore strategies for rebuilding trust and pray for the restoration of a solid foundation in our marriage.

Prayer: Dear God, as we embark on the journey of rebuilding trust, we seek Your guidance and strength. Illuminate the path of restoration, help us to be patient with each other, and grant us the grace to move forward. May our efforts lead to a foundation of trust that is stronger than before. Amen.

Activity: Discuss with your spouse concrete steps you can take together to rebuild trust. This may include setting clear expectations, being consistent in actions, and engaging in activities that foster connection and understanding.

Continue to pray together, seeking God's guidance in every step of this journey toward restoring trust in your marriage.

Day 7-9:
Financial Stress

Money Money Money! It's a universal truth, and let's be honest, saying it doesn't matter would be a bit of a fib. Money matters, and when it comes to marriage, it's like navigating a complex terrain. So, in the days ahead, we're gearing up to explore the landscape of financial stress – digging deep into its roots, discovering strategies to lighten the load, and most importantly, seeking divine wisdom in steering the ship of our finances. Money, the silent player in the game of matrimony, holds the potential for both joy and strife. Through this journey, we aim to unravel its mysteries, finding ways to harmonize our financial life and leaning on God's wisdom to guide us through the twists and turns. Get ready for a deep dive into the realm of dollars and sense – where understanding the roots of financial stress becomes the compass to navigate towards a more peaceful and prosperous future together.

Day 7: Understanding Financial Stress

Financial stress often creeps in when there's a gap between income and expenses or when goals and priorities clash. It's crucial to identify the sources of financial stress in order to address them effectively. On this day, let's reflect on the factors contributing to financial stress in our marriage.

Understanding these dynamics is the first step toward finding solutions and achieving financial peace.

Scriptures:

1. **Proverbs 3:9-10** - "Honor the Lord with your wealth and with the firstfruits of all your produce; then your barns will be filled with plenty, and your vats will be bursting with wine."

2. **Philippians 4:19** - "And my God will supply every need of yours according to his riches in glory in Christ Jesus."

Prayer: Heavenly Father, as we delve into the complexities of financial stress, we seek Your wisdom and understanding. Help us identify the sources of stress and grant us the clarity to make sound financial decisions.

May our finances be aligned with Your will. Amen.

Activity: Have an open conversation with your spouse about the sources of financial stress. Discuss any differences in financial goals and priorities, aiming for a shared understanding.

Day 8: Alleviating Financial Stress

Alleviating financial stress involves practical steps and a mindset shift. It's about finding ways to reduce financial strain and create a more stable financial foundation. On this day, let's explore tips and strategies for easing financial stress, including budgeting, saving, and making intentional choices that align with our financial goals.

Scriptures:

1. **Proverbs 22:7** - "The rich rules over the poor, and the borrower is the slave of the lender."

2. **Matthew 6:21** - "For where your treasure is, there your heart will be also."

Prayer: Lord, we turn to You for guidance in alleviating financial stress. Grant us the discipline to make wise financial choices and the creativity to find solutions. May our hearts be aligned with Your priorities in managing our resources. Amen.

Activity: Together with your spouse, brainstorm and create a budget that reflects your financial goals and priorities. Discuss practical steps to reduce unnecessary expenses and increase savings.

Day 9: Seeking God's Wisdom in Finances

In the realm of finances, seeking God's wisdom is paramount. It involves acknowledging God as the ultimate provider and steward of our resources. On this day, let's explore the importance of seeking God's guidance in financial decisions, including the practice of tithing as a form of obedience and trust in His provision.

Scriptures:

1. **Malachi 3:10** - "Bring the full tithe into the storehouse, that there may be food in my house. And thereby put me to the test, says the Lord of hosts, if I will not open the windows of heaven for you and pour down for you a blessing until there is no more need."

2. **Luke 16:10** - "One who is faithful in a very little is also faithful in much, and one who is dishonest in a very little is also dishonest in much."

Prayer: Dear God, as we explore the significance of seeking Your wisdom in finances, we commit our financial decisions to You. Grant us discernment in managing our resources and the faith to trust in Your provision. May our financial stewardship reflect obedience and honor to You. Amen.

Activity: Discuss with your spouse the role of tithing in your financial journey. Consider ways to incorporate tithing into your budget and financial goals, trusting in God's promise of provision.

Day 10-12:
Lack of Quality Time

In the next few days, let's explore the challenges of lacking quality time in a marriage. We'll delve into understanding how it impacts our spouse, discovering their love language, the significance of quality time, and the role God plays in fostering connection through shared moments.

Day 10: Impact on Your Spouse

Lack of quality time, often experienced uniquely by each spouse, can be a silent intruder in the sanctuary of marriage. It's more than just a clock ticking; it's a significant element influencing emotional and mental landscapes. On this particular day, our journey takes us to reflect on the profound impact of insufficient quality time on our spouse.

The absence of quality time can cast shadows that extend far beyond the surface. It might give rise to feelings of neglect, where the heart longs for a connection that seems elusive. Loneliness may creep in, creating a void that only meaningful time together can fill. The subtle yet poignant sense of not being valued may take root, fostering a yearning for the warmth of shared moments.

Understanding these effects becomes a pivotal milestone on the path to prioritizing and enhancing the time we spend together. It's like deciphering a code – once we comprehend the emotional intricacies, we gain insight into how to mend, nurture, and fortify the bonds that weave our marital tapestry.

In the pursuit of stronger connections, let's embrace the art of quality time, recognizing its power to dispel feelings of neglect, loneliness, and undervaluation. This day marks not just a reflection but a commitment to fostering a deeper, more meaningful togetherness that enriches the very essence of our marriage.

Scriptures:

1. **Ecclesiastes 4:9-10** - "Two are better than one, because they have a good return for their labor: If either of them

falls down, one can help the other up."

2. **1 Corinthians 7:5** - "Do not deprive one another, except perhaps by agreement for a limited time, that you may devote yourselves to prayer; but then come together again, so that Satan may not tempt you because of your lack of self-control."

Prayer: Dear God, as we consider the impact of lacking quality time on our spouse, we seek Your guidance. Open our hearts to understand their needs and grant us the wisdom to prioritize shared moments. May our time together be a source of strength and joy in our marriage. Amen.

Activity: Engage in a heart-to-heart conversation with your spouse about how they feel when quality time is lacking. Create a space for open communication, expressing your willingness to address and improve this aspect of your relationship.

Day 11: Discovering Love Languages

Understanding your spouse's love language is like unlocking a treasure chest of connection and intimacy within your marriage. Gary Chapman's concept of love languages illuminates the unique ways individuals express and receive love – acts of service, words of affirmation, receiving gifts, physical touch, and quality time. On this particular day, we embark on a journey to delve into this invaluable insight and discover our spouse's love language, a key that can significantly elevate the quality of time spent together.

Love languages are the secret codes that speak directly to the heart, transcending mere actions and words. When we grasp the language that resonates most with our spouse, it becomes a compass guiding us towards actions that carry profound meaning and significance. It's not merely about being physically present; it's about aligning our expressions of love with the very essence of what fills their heart.

So, let's set forth on this exploration, asking, observing, and listening to uncover the unique dialect that speaks love to our spouse's soul. It's an investment that pays dividends in the currency of emotional connection, deepening the roots of love and enhancing the quality of every shared moment. As we decode and embrace each other's love language, we open doors to a richer, more fulfilling tapestry of togetherness within the sacred space of our marriage.

Scriptures:

1. **1 Peter 4:8** - "Above all, keep loving one another earnestly, since love covers a multitude of sins."

2. **Song of Solomon 5:16** - "His mouth is most sweet, and he is altogether desirable. This is my beloved and this is my friend."

Prayer: Lord, guide us in discovering and understanding each other's love language. May our actions and words align with the love that strengthens our marriage. Teach us to express love in ways that resonate deeply with our spouse. Amen.

Activity: Explore the love languages with your spouse. Take the Love Language Quiz together and discuss the results. This awareness will guide both of you in expressing love in ways that are meaningful and fulfilling.

Day 12: The Significance of Quality Time

Quality time is more than just being physically present; it is a profound experience of being fully engaged and emotionally present in the moments spent together. As we explore this day, it's an excellent opportunity to uncover the layers of significance that quality time holds within the intricate fabric of our marriage.

Imagine quality time as the handcrafted thread that weaves intimacy, connection, and emotional security into the very fabric of our relationship. It is more than just being in the same room; it is about actively participating, sharing, and creating an environment in which the heart feels seen and heard.

In the hustle of daily life, quality time emerges as a sacred investment, akin to tending to a delicate garden. Each shared moment nurtures the bond between spouses, allowing it to flourish and grow. It fosters a profound sense of togetherness, creating a sanctuary where both partners can find solace, joy, and understanding.

So, let's embrace the depth of this day, recognizing that quality time is not a luxury but a vital component that breathes life into our marriage. It's an intentional choice to prioritize the moments that build a foundation of enduring love, leaving an indelible mark on the canvas of our shared journey.

Scriptures:

1. **Colossians 3:14** - "And above all these put on love, which binds everything together in perfect harmony."

2. **Genesis 2:24** - "Therefore a man shall leave his father and his mother and hold fast to his wife, and they shall become one flesh."

Prayer: Heavenly Father, as we recognize the importance of quality time, we ask for Your guidance. Help us prioritize and cherish the moments we share. May our time together deepen our connection and contribute to the harmony of our marriage. Amen.

"SoulSync: 30 Days of Love and Prayer."

Activity: Plan a special quality time activity with your spouse based on their love language. It could be a date night, a thoughtful gesture, or simply spending undistracted time together. Make a conscious effort to be fully present and engaged during this time.

Day 13-15:
In-Law Conflicts

In the upcoming days, let's navigate the intricate terrain of in-law conflicts within the realm of marriage. This journey invites us to understand the challenges presented and, more importantly, to explore the biblical perspective on these dynamics. As we embark on this exploration, we'll unravel the significance of setting boundaries, seeking God's guidance, and nurturing harmony within extended family relationships.

The Bible, our timeless guide, emphasizes the principle of "leave and cleave." This wisdom, found in Genesis 2:24, speaks to the foundational truth that a man shall leave his father and mother and be joined to his wife, and they shall become one flesh. This biblical directive underscores the importance of prioritizing the marital union and establishing a new family unit.

Genesis 2:24 (NIV): "That is why a man leaves his father and mother and is united to his wife, and they become one flesh."

In-law conflicts often arise when this biblical principle is not upheld, and boundaries between the new couple and their respective families are unclear. Through exploring the challenges and seeking biblical wisdom, we aim to foster a deeper understanding of the "leave and cleave" principle, empowering couples to navigate in-law dynamics with grace, love, and a commitment to the oneness ordained by God.

Day 13: Biblical Perspectives on In-Law Relationships

The Bible offers wisdom on various aspects of life, including relationships with in-laws. Understanding biblical perspectives can provide a solid foundation for navigating in-law conflicts. On this day, let's explore relevant scriptures that shed light on honoring family ties while maintaining the sanctity of the marital relationship.

Scriptures:

1. **Genesis 2:24** - "Therefore a man shall leave his father and his mother and

hold fast to his wife, and they shall become one flesh."

2. **Proverbs 17:17** - "A friend loves at all times, and a brother is born for adversity."

3. **Colossians 3:13** - "Bear with each other and forgive one another if any of you has a grievance against someone. Forgive as the Lord forgave you."

Prayer: Lord, as we consider the biblical perspectives on in-law relationships, we seek Your wisdom. Teach us to honor family ties while nurturing the sacred bond of marriage. May our actions be guided by love, forgiveness, and unity. Amen.

Activity: Read and discuss the scriptures together, reflecting on how they apply to your relationship with in-laws. Identify positive aspects to strengthen and challenging areas that may require prayer and growth.

Day 14: Establishing Boundaries with Love

Setting healthy boundaries is essential for maintaining balance and harmony within extended family relationships. On this day, let's explore the importance of establishing boundaries with love, respecting both the marital union and the connections with in-laws. The goal is to foster understanding and maintain a sense of autonomy while upholding familial bonds.

Scriptures:

1. **Proverbs 4:23** - "Above all else, guard your heart, for everything you do flows from it."

2. **Ephesians 4:2-3** - "Be completely humble and gentle; be patient, bearing with one another in love. Make every effort to keep the unity of the Spirit through the bond of peace."

Prayer: Heavenly Father, guide us as we explore the importance of boundaries within extended family relationships. Grant us the wisdom to establish boundaries with love, humility, and a spirit of unity. May our actions reflect Your grace and maintain the sanctity of our marriage. Amen.

Activity: Discuss and outline boundaries that you and your spouse feel are necessary and respectful in your relationship with in-laws.

Focus on communication and empathy in expressing these boundaries.

Day 15: Seeking God's Guidance in Family Dynamics

Navigating family dynamics, especially in the context of in-law relationships, requires divine guidance. On this day, let's explore the importance of seeking God's wisdom in understanding and addressing family dynamics. By relying on God's guidance, we can navigate conflicts with grace and foster a spirit of harmony.

Scriptures:

1. **James 1:5** - "If any of you lacks wisdom, you should ask God, who gives generously to all without finding fault, and it will be given to you."

2. **Proverbs 3:5-6** - "Trust in the Lord with all your heart and lean not on your own understanding; in all your ways submit to him, and he will make your paths straight."

Prayer: Dear God, as we seek Your guidance in navigating family dynamics, we acknowledge our need for wisdom. Grant us discernment, patience, and understanding as we navigate relationships with in-laws. May Your guidance lead us to resolutions filled with grace and love. Amen.

Activity: Pray together, seeking God's wisdom in specific family dynamics or conflicts. Discuss practical steps to apply biblical principles in your interactions with in-laws, fostering understanding and harmony.

Day 16-18:
Infertility and Family Planning

In the days ahead, let's embark on an emotional journey, shedding light on the challenges couples face in building a family. This exploration invites us to understand the intricate dynamics involved and, more importantly, to delve into the spiritual perspective on this journey. As we navigate this path, we'll unravel the profound significance of seeking God's comfort and guidance, praying for patience, and trusting in His divine timing during the delicate process of family planning.

The Bible, our timeless source of wisdom, encourages us to trust in God's plan and timing. Proverbs 3:5-6 reminds us to "Trust in the Lord with all your heart and lean not on your own understanding; in all your ways submit to him, and he will make your paths straight." This biblical counsel serves as a compass, guiding couples through the emotional complexities of family planning.

Proverbs 3:5-6 (NIV): "Trust in the Lord with all your heart and lean not on your own understanding; in all your ways submit to him, and he will make your paths straight."

Facing the challenges of family planning involves surrendering to God's will, finding solace in His comfort, and patiently awaiting His perfect timing. Through this exploration, we seek to provide insight, encouragement, and a reminder that, even in the midst of challenges, trusting in God's plan brings hope and assurance to the intricate journey of building a family.

Day 16: The Emotional Struggle of Infertility

Infertility can be a deeply emotional struggle for couples longing to build a family. On this day, let's explore the emotional impact of infertility, recognizing the pain, disappointment, and yearning for a child. It's essential to approach this journey with empathy, understanding, and a shared commitment to support one another.

Scriptures:

1. **Psalm 34:18** - "The Lord is near to the brokenhearted and saves the crushed in spirit."

2. **Jeremiah 29:11** - "For I know the plans I have for you, declares the Lord, plans for welfare and not for evil, to give you a future and a hope."

Prayer: Heavenly Father, as we consider the emotional struggle of infertility, we lift up couples facing this challenge. Draw near to those with broken hearts, comforting them in their distress. May Your plans for a hopeful future be a source of strength and solace. Amen.

Activity: Reflect on the emotional aspects of infertility. Share your feelings with your spouse and discuss ways to support each other emotionally during this challenging journey.

Day 17: Seeking God's Comfort and Guidance

In times of uncertainty and heartache, seeking God's comfort and guidance is a source of strength. On this day, let's explore the importance of turning to God for solace and direction during the journey of family planning. Through prayer and reliance on His wisdom, couples can find comfort in knowing that God is intimately involved in their desires for a family.

Scriptures:

1. **Psalm 62:8** - "Trust in him at all times, O people; pour out your heart before him; God is a refuge for us."

2. **Isaiah 41:10** - "Fear not, for I am with you; be not dismayed, for I am your God; I will strengthen you, I will help you, I will uphold you with my righteous right hand."

Prayer: Dear God, as couples navigate the complexities of family planning and infertility, we seek Your comforting presence. Be their refuge and source of strength. Guide them in making decisions that align with Your will. Amen.

Activity: Engage in a joint prayer session with your spouse, pouring out your hearts to God about the challenges and desires related to family planning. Create a space for vulnerability and shared trust in His guidance.

Day 18: Patience and Trust in God's Timing

In the journey of family planning, patience and trust in God's timing become virtues that sustain couples. On this day, let's explore the significance of cultivating patience and trusting in God's sovereign plan. Recognizing that His timing is perfect, couples can find assurance and hope amid the uncertainties of family planning.

Scriptures:

1. **Psalm 27:14** - "Wait for the Lord; be strong, and let your heart take courage; wait for the Lord!"

2. **Proverbs 3:5-6** - "Trust in the Lord with all your heart and lean not on your own understanding; in all your

ways submit to him, and he will make your paths straight."

Prayer: Heavenly Father, grant couples facing challenges in family planning the patience to wait on You and the trust to embrace Your perfect timing. Strengthen their hearts and fill them with hope as they surrender their desires to Your sovereign will. Amen.

Activity: Reflect on the concept of patience and trust in God's timing. Discuss ways to support each other in maintaining a patient and hopeful attitude, keeping faith in the journey ahead.

In these three days, let prayer be a comforting and empowering force, connecting couples with the divine assurance that God walks with them in the journey of family planning and infertility.

Day 19-21:
Emotional Distance

In the days ahead, let's embark on an exploration of the challenges posed by emotional distance within the sacred union of marriage. This journey invites us to understand the origins of emotional distance, explore effective strategies for fostering positive change, and underscore the crucial role of seeking God's guidance in overcoming emotional barriers and rekindling emotional intimacy.

The Bible, our eternal guide, imparts wisdom on the significance of emotional connection. Ephesians 4:2-3 encourages us to "Be completely humble and gentle; be patient, bearing with one another in love. Make every effort to keep the unity of the Spirit through the bond of peace." This biblical counsel serves as a compass, guiding couples through the intricate landscape of emotional distance, urging them to approach each other with humility, patience, and love.

Ephesians 4:2-3 (NIV): "Be completely humble and gentle; be patient, bearing with one another in love. Make every effort to keep the unity of the Spirit through the bond of peace."

Facing emotional distance involves a commitment to positive change, a willingness to understand each other's emotional needs, and a reliance on God's guidance for healing and renewal. Through this exploration, we aim to shed light on the transformative power of seeking God's wisdom, fostering a renewed sense of emotional closeness that strengthens the foundation of marital intimacy.

Day 19: The Genesis of Emotional Distance

Emotional distance can quietly seep into a marriage, often stemming from various factors such as unaddressed conflicts, communication breakdowns, or external stressors. On this day, let's explore how emotional distance starts, acknowledging its subtle beginnings and understanding the potential impact on the marital bond.

Scriptures:

1. **Proverbs 17:9** - "Whoever covers an offense seeks love, but he who repeats a matter separates close friends."

2. **Ephesians 4:26-27** - "In your anger do not sin: Do not let the sun go down while you are still angry, and do not give the devil a foothold."

Prayer: Heavenly Father, as we consider the genesis of emotional distance, we seek Your guidance. Grant us the wisdom to address conflicts promptly and the humility to seek forgiveness when needed. May our hearts be open to love and understanding. Amen.

Activity: Reflect on any recent conflicts or unspoken issues that might contribute to emotional distance. Share your thoughts with your spouse and commit to resolving them together.

Day 20: Changing the Narrative - Strategies for Connection

Positive change begins with intentional efforts to reconnect emotionally. On this day, let's explore practical strategies to change the narrative and foster emotional closeness. From effective communication to shared experiences, these strategies can help rebuild the emotional connection within a marriage.

Scriptures:

1. **1 Corinthians 13:4-7** - "Love is patient, love is kind. It does not envy, it does not boast, it is not proud. It does not dishonor others, it is not self-seeking, it is not easily angered, it

keeps no record of wrongs. Love does not delight in evil but rejoices with the truth. It always protects, always trusts, always hopes, always perseveres."

2. **Colossians 3:14** - "And over all these virtues put on love, which binds them all together in perfect unity."

Prayer: Dear God, guide us as we explore strategies for reconnecting emotionally. Fill our hearts with the virtues of love, patience, and kindness. May our efforts to change the narrative be rooted in Your divine love. Amen.

Activity: Discuss and implement practical strategies for emotional connection, such as setting aside dedicated time for each other, engaging in shared activities, and practicing open communication.

Day 21: Seeking Renewed Emotional Intimacy

Renewing emotional intimacy requires divine guidance and a commitment to vulnerability. On this day, let's explore the significance of seeking God's wisdom in overcoming emotional barriers and fostering a renewed sense of emotional closeness within the marriage.

Scriptures:

1. **Song of Solomon 4:7** - "You are altogether beautiful, my darling; there is no flaw in you."

2. **Philippians 2:2-3** - "Complete my joy by being of the same mind, having the same love, being in full accord

and of one mind. Do nothing from rivalry or conceit, but in humility count others more significant than yourselves."

Prayer: Heavenly Father, as we seek renewed emotional intimacy, we turn to You for guidance. Remove any barriers that hinder our connection and fill our hearts with love and humility. May our marriage be a reflection of Your perfect unity. Amen.

Activity: Engage in a joint prayer session with your spouse, seeking God's guidance in overcoming emotional barriers and fostering renewed emotional intimacy. Share your desires and hopes for a deeper connection.

In these three days, let prayer be the catalyst for change, drawing couples closer emotionally and fostering a renewed sense of intimacy within the marriage.

Day 22-24:
Power Struggles

In the days ahead, let's navigate the intricate dynamics of power struggles within the sacred bond of marriage. This exploration delves into the complexities of why these conflicts arise, how they take root, and underscores the profound significance of seeking God's guidance in resolving them. Couples are encouraged to cultivate humility, find common ground through compromises, and establish a harmonious division of responsibilities – all grounded in the transformative power of prayer.

The Bible, our timeless source of wisdom, illuminates the importance of humility and unity. Philippians 2:3-4 counsels us to "Do nothing out of selfish ambition or vain conceit. Rather, in humility, value others above yourselves, not looking to your own interests but each of you to the interests of the others." This biblical insight serves as a guiding light, urging couples to approach power struggles with a spirit of humility and a commitment to mutual understanding.

Philippians 2:3-4 (NIV): "Do nothing out of selfish ambition or vain conceit. Rather, in humility, value others above yourselves, not looking to your own interests but each of you to the interests of the others."

Addressing power struggles involves a willingness to seek common ground, make compromises, and find a balanced and harmonious distribution of responsibilities through the transformative act of prayer. Through this exploration, we aim to provide insight and encouragement, highlighting the transformative impact of seeking God's guidance in navigating the delicate terrain of power dynamics within marriage.

Day 22: The Significance of Addressing Power Struggles

Power struggles matter in a marriage because they can create tension, hinder effective communication, and erode the foundation of trust and intimacy. On this day, let's explore why addressing power struggles is crucial. Understanding the impact of these conflicts allows couples to navigate them with intentionality and a commitment to mutual growth.

Scriptures:

1. **Philippians 2:3-4** - "Do nothing out of selfish ambition or vain conceit. Rather, in humility, value others above yourselves, not looking to your interests but each of you to the interests of the others."

2. **Ephesians 5:21** - "Submit to one another out of reverence for Christ."

Prayer: Dear God, as we consider the significance of addressing power struggles, we seek Your guidance. Instill in us the virtues of humility and selflessness, that we may navigate conflicts with a spirit of unity and mutual respect. Amen.

Activity: Reflect on recent power struggles within your marriage. Discuss the impact they may have had on your relationship and commit to addressing them with a spirit of humility and understanding.

Day 23: Understanding the Genesis of Power Struggles

Power struggles often emerge from differences in expectations, communication styles, or unmet needs. On this day, let's explore how these conflicts begin, acknowledging the various factors that contribute to the genesis of power struggles. Understanding the root causes is essential for effective resolution.

Scriptures:

1. **James 4:1-2** - "What causes fights and quarrels among you? Don't they

come from your desires that battle within you? You desire but do not have, so you kill. You covet but you cannot get what you want, so you quarrel and fight."

2. **Proverbs 15:1** - "A gentle answer turns away wrath, but a harsh word stirs up anger."

Prayer: Heavenly Father, guide us as we explore the genesis of power struggles within our marriage. Grant us insight into the root causes and help us address them with wisdom and love. May our conflicts lead to growth and understanding. Amen.

Activity: Engage in a conversation with your spouse about the factors that may contribute to power struggles. Listen actively and seek mutual understanding as you explore the root causes together.

Day 24: Seeking God's Guidance for Resolution

Resolving power struggles requires divine guidance and a commitment to finding compromises. On this day, let's explore the importance of seeking God's wisdom in navigating conflicts within the marriage. Through prayer, couples can find the strength to overcome power struggles, fostering compromises and mutual understanding.

Scriptures:

1. **Proverbs 3:5-6** - "Trust in the Lord with all your heart and lean not on your own understanding; in all your

ways submit to him, and he will make your paths straight."

2. **Colossians 3:13** - "Bear with each other and forgive one another if any of you has a grievance against someone. Forgive as the Lord forgave you."

Prayer: Dear God, as we seek Your guidance in resolving power struggles, we surrender our conflicts to You. Grant us the wisdom to find compromises and the humility to forgive. May our marriage reflect the grace and forgiveness You have shown us. Amen.

Activity: Pray together, seeking God's guidance in specific power struggles you may be facing. Discuss practical steps to find compromises, forgive one another, and foster mutual understanding.

In these three days, let prayer be the cornerstone for addressing power struggles, cultivating humility, and seeking God's wisdom to navigate conflicts within the marriage.

Day 25-27:
Addiction Issues

In the upcoming days, let's embark on a journey to understand the challenges posed by addiction within the sacred bond of marriage. This exploration delves into the complexities of addiction, discussing the vital importance of praying for deliverance, seeking God's strength to overcome addictive behaviors, and cultivating a supportive environment conducive to healing.

The Bible, our timeless guide, offers wisdom on the power of prayer and divine strength. Philippians 4:13 assures us that "I can do all things through Christ who strengthens me." This biblical truth becomes a cornerstone, guiding couples through the challenging terrain of addiction, reminding them of the transformative strength found in seeking God's intervention.

Philippians 4:13 (NIV): "I can do all things through Christ who strengthens me."

Addressing addiction involves a joint commitment to prayer, drawing on God's strength to break free from the chains of addictive behaviors. Creating a supportive environment becomes a crucial aspect of this journey, fostering understanding, compassion, and a space for healing. Through this exploration, we seek to shed light on the transformative power of seeking God's guidance in navigating the complexities of addiction within the sacred context of marriage.

Day 25: The Impact of Addiction on Marriage

Addiction can cast a shadow over a marriage, affecting trust, communication, and overall well-being. On this day, let's explore the impact of addiction on the marital relationship. Understanding the consequences is essential for approaching the journey to recovery with empathy and commitment.

Scriptures:

1. **1 Corinthians 6:12** - "I have the right to do anything," you say—but not everything is beneficial. "I have the

right to do anything"—but I will not be mastered by anything."

2. **Philippians 4:13** - "I can do all this through him who gives me strength."

Prayer: Heavenly Father, as we consider the impact of addiction on marriage, we seek Your guidance. Grant us the strength to face the challenges ahead and the wisdom to approach recovery with love and understanding. Amen.

Activity: Reflect on how addiction has impacted your marriage. Engage in an open and honest conversation with your spouse, acknowledging the challenges and committing to support each other through the journey to recovery.

Day 26: Praying for Deliverance

Prayer becomes a powerful tool in seeking deliverance from addiction. On this day, let's explore the significance of fervently praying for deliverance from any form of addiction affecting the marriage. Turning to God in prayer invites His transformative power into the process of healing and recovery.

Scriptures:

1. **Psalm 34:17-18** - "The righteous cry out, and the Lord hears them; he delivers them from all their troubles. The Lord is close to the brokenhearted and saves those who are crushed in spirit."

2. **James 5:16** - "Therefore confess your sins to each other and pray for each other so that you may be healed. The

prayer of a righteous person is powerful and effective."

Prayer: Dear God, as we pray for deliverance from addiction, we lift our hearts to You. Hear our cries, and deliver us from the grip of any form of addiction affecting our marriage. Grant us the strength to overcome, and may Your healing power bring restoration. Amen.

Activity: Engage in a joint prayer session with your spouse, confessing any struggles with addiction and seeking deliverance. Create a safe space for vulnerability and support.

Day 27: Seeking God's Strength for Overcoming

Overcoming addiction requires inner strength, and seeking God's strength is foundational to the journey of recovery. On this day, let's explore the importance of relying on God's strength to overcome addictive behaviors. Through faith, couples can find the resilience needed for lasting transformation.

Scriptures:

1. **2 Corinthians 12:9-10** - "But he said to me, 'My grace is sufficient for you, for my power is made perfect in weakness.' Therefore I will boast all the more gladly about my weaknesses, so that Christ's power may rest on me."

2. **Isaiah 41:10** - "So do not fear, for I am with you; do not be dismayed, for I am your God. I will strengthen you

and help you; I will uphold you with my righteous right hand."

Prayer: Heavenly Father, as we seek Your strength to overcome addiction, we recognize our weakness. Fill us with Your grace and empower us with the resilience needed for lasting transformation. Be our source of strength, O Lord. Amen.

Activity: Reflect on the scriptures that emphasize God's strength in overcoming challenges. Discuss with your spouse how relying on His strength can become a cornerstone in your journey to recovery.

In these three days, let prayer be the foundation for addressing addiction issues, seeking deliverance, and relying on God's strength for lasting transformation within the marriage.

Day 28-30:
Unresolved Past Trauma and Role Expectations

As we near the end of this prayerful journey, let's explore the intricate complexities of unresolved past trauma and the profound impact of role expectations within the sacred covenant of marriage. This exploration delves into the importance of praying for healing from past traumas, seeking God's guidance in establishing realistic role expectations, and fervently praying for a marriage based on grace, forgiveness, and alignment with God's divine plan.

The Bible, our eternal source of wisdom, imparts guidance on healing and forgiveness. Psalm 147:3 assures us that "He heals the brokenhearted and binds up their wounds." This biblical truth serves as a beacon of hope, guiding couples through the delicate process of healing from past traumas, reminding them that God's transformative power can mend even the deepest wounds.

Psalm 147:3 (NIV): "He heals the brokenhearted and binds up their wounds."

Setting realistic role expectations within marriage is illuminated by the guidance found in Romans 12:2, urging us to "not conform to the pattern of this world, but be transformed by the renewing of your mind." This biblical principle becomes a cornerstone, guiding couples to seek God's wisdom in defining roles within their union, fostering understanding, and aligning expectations with His divine plan.

Romans 12:2 (NIV): "Do not conform to the pattern of this world, but be transformed by the renewing of your mind."

In the final days of our journey, let's pray fervently for healing, wisdom, and a marriage grounded in grace and forgiveness. May our roles within this sacred union be shaped by God's divine plan, paving the way for a future filled with unity, understanding, and enduring love.

Day 28: Praying for Healing from Past Traumas

Unresolved past traumas can cast a long shadow over a marriage, affecting emotional well-being and intimacy. On this day, let's explore the significance of praying for healing from past traumas and wounds. Turning to God in prayer invites His transformative power into the process of healing and restoration.

Scriptures:

1. **Psalm 147:3** - "He heals the brokenhearted and binds up their wounds."

2. **Isaiah 61:1** - "The Spirit of the Sovereign Lord is on me, because the Lord has anointed me to proclaim good news to the poor. He has sent me to bind up the brokenhearted, to proclaim freedom for the captives and

release from darkness for the prisoners."

Prayer: Dear God, as we pray for healing from past traumas, we entrust our brokenness to You. Heal our hearts, bind up our wounds, and bring restoration to the places where we carry pain. May Your Spirit bring freedom and release from the darkness of past traumas. Amen.

Activity: Engage in a joint prayer session with your spouse, expressing any past traumas that may still affect you. Create a space for vulnerability and support as you seek healing together.

Day 29: Seeking God's Guidance in Setting Realistic Role Expectations

Role expectations within a marriage can sometimes lead to misunderstandings and unmet needs. On this day, let's explore the importance of seeking God's guidance in setting realistic role expectations. Aligning roles with God's plan fosters understanding, flexibility, and a shared commitment to mutual growth.

Scriptures:

1. **Proverbs 3:5-6** - "Trust in the Lord with all your heart and lean not on your own understanding; in all your ways submit to him, and he will make your paths straight."

2. **Ephesians 5:21** - "Submit to one another out of reverence for Christ."

Prayer: Heavenly Father, guide us as we seek Your wisdom in setting realistic role expectations within our marriage. Help us submit to one another with reverence for

Christ, fostering a spirit of understanding and mutual support. Amen.

Activity: Discuss with your spouse the roles and expectations each of you brings to the marriage. Seek God's guidance in aligning these expectations with His plan, promoting mutual understanding and growth.

Day 30: Praying for a Marriage Built on Grace, Forgiveness, and God's Plan

As we conclude this 30-day prayer journey, let's focus on praying for a marriage built on foundational principles of grace, forgiveness, and alignment with God's plan. These elements form the bedrock of a resilient and thriving marital relationship.

Scriptures:

1. **Colossians 3:13** - "Bear with each other and forgive one another if any

of you has a grievance against someone. Forgive as the Lord forgave you."

2. **Proverbs 19:21** - "Many are the plans in a person's heart, but it is the Lord's purpose that prevails."

Prayer: Dear God, as we pray for our marriage, we seek Your grace and forgiveness. May our relationship be built on the foundation of Your love, with a commitment to aligning our plans with Yours. Guide us in Your purpose for our marriage. Amen.

Activity: Engage in a joint prayer session with your spouse, expressing gratitude for the 30-day journey and committing your marriage to God's plan. Discuss practical ways to incorporate grace and forgiveness into your daily interactions.

In these final three days, let prayer be the guiding force for healing from past traumas, setting realistic role expectations, and building a marriage grounded in grace, forgiveness, and God's plan. May this journey strengthen your connection and bring lasting transformation to your marital relationship.

Closing Note to Readers

Dear Readers,

As we come to the end of this 30-day journey, we want to express our deepest gratitude to you. Thank you for joining us on this exploration of prayer, love, and the intricacies of marriage. Your presence and commitment to growth and understanding in your own relationships mean the world to us.

We hope the words within these pages have touched your hearts, provided insights, and sparked meaningful reflections. Marriage is a journey, and we're honored to have shared a part of it with you. May the wisdom gained from these prayers and reflections bring a positive impact to your life and relationships.

Remember, love is a continuous journey, and we wish you abundant blessings, joy, and a love that grows stronger with each passing day.

With heartfelt thanks,

David Hassan Habbi Love

and Dr. Lashawnda Love

Meet the Authors

David Love

David Hassan Habbi Love is an esteemed author, ordained Deacon, and community activist known for his commitment to positive transformation and empowerment. In September 2023, he achieved the significant milestone of ordination as a Deacon at Kingdom Ambassador Ministries under the guidance of Apostle Delesa Patterson. Alongside this accomplishment, David has authored impactful books, including "Unleash the

"SoulSync: 30 Days of Love and Prayer."

Power Within, Break Free, and Embrace a Transformed Life," and "30 Days of Transformation: Overcoming Addiction and Embracing a New Life." This practical and faith-based devotional serves as a comprehensive guide, offering daily exercises, prayers, and practical applications for lasting transformation.

Adding to his repertoire, David, together with his wife Lashawnda Love, has recently released their collaborative work, "SoulSync: 30 Days of Love and Prayer." This latest book is a testament to their dedication to promoting love and spirituality through a 30-day journey of prayer and reflection.

David Love is also the visionary founder of Boys to Kings, a mentorship program aimed at empowering young boys to become leaders. His inspiring journey is chronicled in the book "How I Went from Arrested to Rescued," where he shares his story of finding hope and transformation through faith during 19 years of imprisonment.

Alongside his literary contributions, David and Lashawnda have introduced "The Loves Collection," featuring journals and T-shirts that reflect their creativity and commitment to empowering others. NBQ Kings Edition Magazine has recognized David for his outstanding dedication to mentoring and empowering the next generation of leaders.

As a community activist, David dedicates his time and resources to various causes, including advocating for criminal justice reform and supporting local youth programs. He exemplifies the positive impact one person can make through perseverance, faith, and a heart for service.

David Love's story serves as a beacon of hope, reminding us that even in the darkest moments, there is always the potential for a brighter future. His books, including the latest "SoulSync," offer inspiration and encouragement on the journey toward personal growth and transformation.

To connect with David Love, you can reach him via email at davidhassanlove@gmail.com or visit his website at https://bit.ly/3YUzvy9 for more information about his work and upcoming events. David is also active on social media, where you can find him on Facebook as Dahoo MrNewYork Love, on Instagram as

David and Lashawnda Love, and on TikTok as David Love. Stay up-to-date with his latest projects and connect with him directly through these platforms.

Whether you're interested in Boys to Kings, supporting his community activism, or exploring the transformative power of his books, David Love welcomes your message and looks forward to connecting with you.

Lashawnda Love

Lashawnda Shiree Love is a multi-talented individual with a wide range of skills and expertise. She is the devoted wife of David Hassan Habbi Love and a loving mother of three children - Chadrick Kyles Jr,

"SoulSync: 30 Days of Love and Prayer."

23, Shedrick Kyles, 18, and Purpose Lamb, 9. Lashawnda is an entrepreneur, business owner, minister, community service provider, author, ghostwriter, YouTube Vlogger, make-up artist, and gospel recording artist.

Lashawnda wears many hats, including CEO of Intellectual Designs by Lashawnda Love (Social Media Marketing), where she creates websites, social media content, and social media training. She has created magazines for Mogul Leaders Magazine, N.B.Q Magazine, and numerous graphics for K.I.S.H. Magazine. Additionally, she has her own cosmetics line called "Lashawnda Shiree," which features over 16 different shades of 16-hour matte lipsticks and 2 lip liners.

"SoulSync: 30 Days of Love and Prayer."

Lashawnda is also a life coach and mentor, holding a Doctorate in Christian Counseling, a master's in Psychology, and currently pursuing a Clinical Mental Health degree at GCU. She serves as a therapist and Program Manager at the Heritage Foundation of Thomasville, GA. Lashawnda is the visionary behind B.A.B.Y. Ministry (Becoming A Better You). Her passion is for souls to be saved, marriages to be healed, and chains to be broken.

She recently birthed a publishing company called "Stork Publishing LLC," and she and her husband have also created journals and a T-shirt line called "The Loves Collection." Lashawnda is a multi-talented individual with a diverse range of accomplishments. As a gifted singer and songwriter, she has produced several soul-stirring singles, including "Deeper," "The Perfect Gift," and "Silent Night." In the literary realm, she authored impactful books and spearheaded the Prophetic Release "Prayer for the Nations" CD, showcasing her deep spiritual commitment. Her literary works encompass titles such as "Put Your Cat on the Altar," "B.A.B.Y Magazine," "There is Power when a Wife Prays!", "Make Your Marriage Better (a free ebook)," "A Guide to Winning the War Against a Narcissist," "Rock Your Spouse World 7 Days out of the Month," and "A Girl's Guide to Purity" (co-authored with Dr. Erica Thomas). She has also ghostwritten her husband's book, "How I Went from Arrested to Rescued." The latest addition to her literary repertoire is the co-authored book with her husband, David Love, titled

"SoulSync: 30 Days of Love and Prayer." Her agenda, "Just a Girl Who Survived and Decided to Build Her Empire," stands as a testament to her resilience.

Lashawnda is also a divorce coach, using her personal experiences to help others navigate the difficult process of ending a marriage. She owns an in-home catering company called Mama Tees Catering, where she provides healthy keto meal preps.

Lashawnda's goal is to promote the kingdom of God through praise and worship, help broken and battered women, and continue to "let my light shine!" She has declared that every year she will be birthing every vision that God has given her, and the sky is genuinely the limit.

Connect with Lashawnda on various media platforms: Facebook (Lashawnda Love), Facebook Business Page (Intellectual Designs by Lashawnda Love), Instagram (LashawndaShireeLove), YouTube (Lashawnda Shiree Love), TikTok (Dr Lashawndalove), Clubhouse (@LashawndaLamb), via email (llove@lashawndashiree.info), or by phone (334-232-9281). Visit her websites: www.lashawndashiree.info, www.payhip/lashawndashiree, www.lovescollection.com, and bit.ly/3UGzLOo.

Download her music on Pandora, Amazon, Spotify, and Deezer.

www.ingramcontent.com/pod-product-compliance
Lightning Source LLC
Chambersburg PA
CBHW052057150726
48002CB00002B/930